MOONLIGHT ON WORDS

The third selection of twenty-four poems by the finest poetical voice of the post-war generation of English poets.

'She's brilliant.'

Roy MacGregor Hastie

Further selections of poems by Shänne Sands

- Vol.1   Fidelity Is For Swans
- Vol.2   The Silver Hooves
- Vol.4   Night Song
- Vol.5   Fragments Of Desire

MOONLIGHT ON WORDS

Selected Poems By
SHÄNNE SANDS
Volume 3

❖

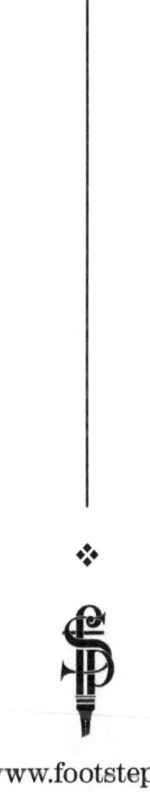

www.footsteps.co

© Shänne Sands 2012

The right of Shänne Sands to be identified as the author of this work and illustrations has been asserted in accordance with sections 77 and 78 of the copyright designs and patents act 1988.

Moonlight On Words

Footsteps Press first edition
www.footsteps.co

Cover design by Kevin Reilly and
Jackie Pascoe

Typeset by Jackie Pascoe

Set in century
ISBN 978-0-9566349-8-6

Reproduction of any or all of this work in any form, electronic or otherwise, is expressly forbidden without the prior contractual agreement of the author. Incidental illustrations are taken from the original hand written volumes by Shänne Sands.

To Daddy

Incidental illustrations from the original hand written scripts

POEMS

Parnassus	1
Where Leaps the Flame	2
The Day Of A Cunning Careerist	3
The Dark Island	4
Across The Borders Of It All	5
Of Poems	6
Defeat	7
A Tall Man Like A Tree	8
On A Lock Of Keats' Hair In A Texas College	10
Beyond The Wind And The Rain	11
Underneath the Arches Of My Mind	13
Swan Time	15
The Suffering Now	17
Finis	18
Watching The Rain At Treknow	21
Art	22
Family Meeting On Liskeard Station	23
Song Of The Red Sail	25
Necessitas	27
Winter	28
Man Is A Bundle Of Ash	29
Emily Brontë	30
Whispers	31
The Faded Leaf	32

Parnassus

All pretence is over now,
Over the other side of me,
The me that has been barely stripped of every promise.
Fables are left
Where at a certain time, some could find such a truth
Large and alive,
Alas, too filled with a hope
That hardly could survive.
Ugliness, more deformed than his name
Blasted upon the sweetness of living.
Came and gone
Is the one to forgive,
Left near me is the unforgiving.
Rival attitudes distract the mind,
Pernicious cupids bring poison
Where love could but die.
Treasures collected with the fondness of youth
Are left in cardboard boxes
Tied with sordid string by the hands of the uncouth.
Then there are letters
Sent by strangers turned friends,
Whose characters cross and tangle with new days.
The old days
Now immemorial.
An unfinished poem insults the fame I seek,
Parnassus, no more speaks.

Where Leaps The Flame

If this poem was an element,
It would be fire -
A million scarlet tongues
Would be its flame
Each hot flicker to proclaim
A martyr's name.

Not martyrs of the Cross
They are re-born in stone
But martyrs of camps of hell
All unknown, un-named
Shall in this poem
Be crowned with flame

The atoms from each soul
Will fly the unknown tombs
Fire and flame raised from bone
Even beyond eternity -
Free to the outer-rim of space and time -
Sings the martyr's cause
Now yours and mine.
Each name spelt out from fire
This poem not of desire, but honour
Mercy, love, where leaps the flame.

THE DAY OF A CUNNING CAREERIST

He learnt at an early age
To deliver taxed dreams
To his breakfast table,
Where he shared the fruit-juice and the papers
With his wife -
Spreading marmalade with
A small silver knife on their
Thinly sliced toast -
Bitter-orange marmalade to match
Their bitter orange destiny -
Listening to the news -
Rushing into the day believing it
To be important -
Driving over flyovers -
A quick drink with Tom
Wondering where his favourite tart had gone -
Her address lay sprawled in his diary -
The one he kept at the office
Under a pile of 'Time & Tide' and the
'Country Gentleman'
The devil you will find is a snob -
Whose club is somewhere off Charing-Cross -
As a tax is put on fornication, dreams,
New rugs and that drug which keeps
Youth locked into old men's groins
And lets fading women rich and vain
Believe they can be young again -
False declarations of courage and love -
Falls from the cunning careerist's lips -
As he eyes a woman he wants for the night -
Yet with surprise she leaves abruptly -
While he's still coughing out his words -
Then his ardent breath smelling
Of too much Guinness almost stops
His throat up -
She didn't hear a word - and he is furious -
Not being able to hatch his sex
Out of himself into her -
But he bends like a green sharp reed
And decides to catch the last train home -

THE DARK ISLAND
(FOR ANTHONY)

When we go dearest
To the faraway-land -
Soft music will sing us
Along the shores of the dark island -
We'll call the island home or love
Or God - no devils there, only you
Stroking my hair and me kissing
Your fingers -

Our poems will be songs for the gulls -
Heather will bind our lips with mountain-air
And cares will drop into the sea -
Lost forever - we'll dance - skip
To our tune and a haze of gold
Will circle our island days -

When we go to the faraway-land -
Your black-thoughts will turn
To silver-bells, that you can hang
Around my ears -
I'll sport your ring
And love you till death -

Ride to the dark island with me -
Where wild passions will
Rule our nights -
And sleep is but to wake to love
Near all that's free -
All the gods allow on Earth -
Fresh, pure wind -
And rain across our skins -
Above us a sky of stars
With our love its sun -
Come my dearest to
The faraway-land - come.

ACROSS THE BORDERS OF IT ALL

I know that one day I shall fall
Across the borders of it all -

Complete choice of beauty's skill -
Nearness, promise, forward thrill -

Cast out, destroy empty havoc -
Immerse those mock

Rude tongues in burning oil -
Across the borders of it all!

Of Poems

Being a poet
A maker
I must make
A poem from a clothes-line -
From dry sticks
I must make flower-poems
Grow and bend
And smell of life -

From goodbye
I must make - as a poet does -
Tears that sing
Tunes of pleasure -
I must make a poem of grief
Even if my poem becomes
A worded thief full of
Promises it cannot keep -

A maker is a brief creator
Burnt-out in nerve and tissue
But from age I must make
As a maker does, poems
That cling to life
And in the ice-cold morning
Of the new poems break-thro'
I must make a pool of healing -
For miracles are poems too -

Treading the air and the ground
I shed my poems, now flowers
For the birds to swallow and sing-up
On a bleak dawn near to some new-born
Poor thing that weeps from birth -
I must make a poem of that birth
And hang it on the clothes-line to dry

❖

DEFEAT

I have no words to howl into your ears
About my love - how it fears
Destruction in its dreams which
Ransack all thoughts and stitch
My heart to your shirts -
Lying on my bed - counting all my hurts -
With your cuff-links - I try to
Dally with the acquiescence needed for loving you -
But it is not possible to love this way -
If you forbid me to lay
Myself near your feet -
I am a prisoner in dull defeat -
Listening while you concoct excuses like tulips
In parks stiffly organized and whip
Them about my brain -
I'll expunge you from the rain
That drips and drops outside all I feel
Remembering once you were real.

A Tall Man Like A Tree

Long ago I loved a man
Tall like a tree -

With a wave
Or two
In his hair -

Eyes blue
As heaven -
Skin fair -

Long-fingered hands
Rather funny ears
Legs of a stallion
Kiss of a rogue

Time wears
Lovers out
Little by little

Only voices
Ring a familiar
Chime -

Now I love
A tall man

With hair
Grey here
And there -

Eyes tired
Hands slightly
Worn -

Still rather
Funny ears
Still legs
Of a stallion
Kiss of a rogue -

Age is in
The eyes
Of the beholder

And I can only see

A man tall
Like a tree
With a wave
Or two in his hair -

Eyes blue
As heaven
Skin fair -
With rather
Funny ears -

An evergreen-man like a tree

ON A LOCK OF KEATS' HAIR IN A TEXAS COLLEGE

Poor dear Keats your hair, silken red-gold still -
As Leigh Hunt snipped that lock with kind respect -
Long ago, were you standing on a hill?
Your weak chest aching from pale love's neglect -
As Leigh Hunt spied your glittering hair sun-bright -
And for us kept this strand of silken poetry -
With other poets' hair, who flew like kites
Their thoughts across heaven to set us free -
Now, in a Texas college this relic stays
For American students to glance at -
Keats would not have understood their modern ways -
Their 'sophistication' would leave him flat -
   Beneath a Texas moon, no high Greek song is sung -
   Keats' red-gold hair is wound around an English tongue.

Beyond The Wind And The Rain
(For Daddy)

With the wind against your back you died -
With the sunlight in my eyes I cried -
Your dying was a poor man's death -
Your last words spoken with a
Poor man's breath -
My grief was honest loving
For your bones -
Turned too soon on a 9th day
To cold stone -
   Ah! What ailed you father mine
   Ah! What failed you father dear
   Was the air too cold
   The wind too wild
   Or the day too damp
   And the hill too steep
   So now you sleep
   So now I weep -

Beyond the wind and the rain -
Beyond your pain -
Beyond your struggle -
   Little hands pray
   Little voices sing
   Little poems wait -

Pity was in your eyes
Laughter in your talk
Fun in your walk
Hands that were wise -

Death takes everything
And yet takes nothing -
Here is your summer
Here is your sea
Listen to your music
Listen to your footsteps -

Your burial place
Has no head stone
No vase of flowers
No words of cold-death -

This is your epitaph -
"Here lies my father -

A small man with a strong voice -
His life was a climb towards the stars
And he called them diamonds
And loved their glitter -
   He suffered -
   He was a Jew -
   He was loved like the sunshine."

Ah! Father mine ailing and old -
Ah! Father dear your life is told -
Beyond your grave
Beyond your dust -
   See the gulls are free
   See the day is warm
   See the storm is over.

Underneath The Arches Of My Mind

Underneath the arches of my mind
Against the small white bricks of thought
And unkind dusty walls,
My indifference brushed my
Boredom with sorrow -
I turned from my precious visions
Because suddenly I was sightless
To their pictures gently balanced
High above my shattered hopes -

In the tree-high shrubbery of Self
A phantom-Elf danced a dance of torment
And with every dainty step he skipped
He stole away from me another day -

From this bare-wayside
I have to plant seeds -
Make them grow
Even pray for rain
In a cold climate -

I could not allow the Elf to win
His was a dance of death and decay
I was a child of the month of May -

Narrow brain cells gave me headaches
People in the shape of fallen leaves
Betrayed the ground they fell upon -
And were not re-born -

Small light angels
Sang an occasional chant
I joined in the chorus
When I remembered the words -

A fiend called poverty
Essential to the poet's need
Made of me a statue
Caste in iron -
Boiled in fire -
Then painted gold and dipped in blood -
As the twilight of anguish turned to night
My plight seemed less like doom
But more like a rising new-moon

Over my favourite hills -

Music played on my heart
Softer sounds than love -
A pensive hour gave me purer reason -
Pain made me lie still
And cease from the run and tumble
Of those around me -
An old windmill was pretty -
My nearness to the earth
Always pleased me -

Damage to my ideals was inevitable
They were to be broken -
I was to be chastised -

There is an eternal promise
In the fields around a house -
A Christ in every grain of wheat
A possible sweet progress
In standing still -
Swiftly years die, but patience
Is a slow walk towards
The inner Self-will -
Where rebellion
Is very hard to put down -

Swan Time

The white swan
And the black swan
And the lake
Their dreams
Float upon.

Then the soft winds
Then the ugly winds -
Then the tumbled feathers -
Then the million leaves -

Suddenly the cold seas -
The unkind waves
And soon the warm seas
And soon the softest sands -

Even a few hills
Even a tangled wood
The understood message
Of an old tree-stump.

Higher still than cloud
A fragment of moon -
Then the call of space
Then the quest of stars
Then the dark silence -

Morning-rise -
Daytime-rise -
Evening closing-in-buttercups -
Bees on manoeuvres -
Goodnight to tall grasses -
The dryness and
The wetness and
The mean time and
The happy time and
The smiling second and
The crying second and
The wonder second.

Then the house image
Then the swaying hopes -
Then the complete walk
Then the complete talk -

Suddenly a tiny wren,
Then again swans -
Then again lakes -

Then again dreams -
Then suddenly to wake -
Again a breeze
Again sea filled shells -
Again the scent of wonder -

The Suffering Now

Suffering of the Now -
Kills in spirit
The body saved from
The last war -
This is the spoil for new armies
Falling bombs missed the delicate
Child with sweet hands -
Who grew into lovely woman
In the suffering Now
Ready for rape -
Sickness is not only death
Cruelty is not only man -
Beneath a laughing sky
Political germs spread the agony
Of the Cross -
Answers escape like bullets
Through a skull -
Shrilling it is never enough to die -
Whilst your country's flag
Waves in the senile breeze -
Above your graves-dead youths -
Paved with your mothers' tears -
Noble in foreign soil
You all rot -
March to live -
Strike out perverted hate -
With clean, young hands -
Remember why men died -
Do not allow the sperming of H-bombs -
Or 'fall-outs' to sprinkle death
Through the blood -
March to Freedom's wanting song -
Singing of camps
And bleeding hearts -
Of Mans' suffering,
Let pity whip your mind -
As you realize
Against your youth
War will always try
To score a huge success!

FINIS

A flowering cactus droops
It's flame red flower -
Bursting with blood -
From a dry soil, hardly needing water -
Only a food of old stale matter -
Yellow or dungish looking -

Somehow all so much like
An old dry intellect -
Stale with too much used wit
And odd theories -
Too many lies woven out of bad situations
On inauspicious days -
Drooped with deceit -
Bent with modern satire -
Striking at the heart
And at the ear -

I found you once, beside a flooded river -
Full as the sun and shining
Like my opal ring -
All blues and pinks, as mad, gay
Glints of fire - left that bright stone
And touched your blue eyes -
Eyes that were still young -
Still mine.
Our love trembled on the steps -
And leapt from a double-bed -
Onto the floor -
Where your hands led the stars
From heaven to my feet -

Time bled you of promise -
A wife unloved, unwanted, but like
A germ crept around your life ('till divorce)
And bit with sour-vine-juice
Into your spleen -

Time is not cruel
It's there to live -
But a corrupt finger
Takes the purple truth
And dyes it black -
In silence we creep to face

A flight of broken stairs -
Pretending we don't give a damn
For lies or pale deceit -
Then we weep -

Yet this hurt is real -
This unpleasant reason
Is a jagged knife -
Double-edged and full of ruby blood -
Both yours and mine -

You 'broke my heart'
Bent a kiss in half -
Tore apart our dreams and fled -
But when the day is past
And one by one timeless stars appear
Then you and I alone, hand in hand -
Face this open mirror
And see ourselves as we really are -
You are not scarred with living spit -
A male-whore climbing over lust -
I am not desolate with dreams -
We are one -
Turned from our stone -
Into flesh and blood -
We live -
We live -
And then the mirror cracks -
Glass cuts my face -
And I
Forgive
Forgive -

Of Earth's joys love
Is most betrayed -
From Earth's woe
Love weeps loudest -

Age packs us-up
Into fragments of dust -
As we reap seeds our love has sown -
So I saw you once
Beside your own disguise
Of words and jest -

I saw you naked and asleep -
Now I'll forget the ancient germ -
That festers in your guts -
And makes you weak!
And remember that once you said
In your half-sleep naked and warm
Near my arms 'I love you"
That is enough for gods to save -

On this windy day of early spring -
Let vice and lies tread the outside streets
I'll take a slow retreat
With those few words -
And live within their charm -
Leap to my sight
Your sleeping face -
And hear your voice in dreams -

WATCHING THE RAIN AT TREKNOW

If you ever watch the rain
Sweep across a great high plain
Of damp green fields and bent-backward trees,
Where seagulls' wings are taut with breeze,
And gusts of wind cut you in half
Near a Cornish cow and her soft calf -
Almost blown across a field -
Where it seems impossible to build
Cottages of bleak grey stone
That become warm home sweet home -
Then you will know as well as I,
How the sunset warms the sky
When the rain stops and the wind stops -
And an autumn evening drops
Darkness all around -
And there's never a sound -
Over the great high plain -
All is quiet in West-country lanes -
Only the hedgerow high, wild and free -
Hides the horizon and masks the sea -
That sends the winds across the plain -
And lets you watch Treknow's grey rain.

          (TINTAGEL, CORNWALL)

ART

This is a life,
Where poet, writer, painter,
Heat their hands from flames
Burning from the brain's fire -
Earth's very sky is held still
As they turn sea to words -
Rock to paint -
Wine and beer wash throats
With song and conversation -
In a bodily exchange for art -
Where to belong you climb a broken ladder
And give to words, paint, music, dance
A fire-washed agonised-pure soul -
Creation banged out of marble
Poems burning from a special womb -
Covering every last thought
With chalk-white burnt-out dust -
Until a huge soft pile smothers you
Into a deep and grateful sleep -

(AFTER AN EARLY LUNCH ONE SUNDAY, NOV 1963 WITH POETS PAINTER, JOURNALIST. LAMORNA COVE, CORNWALL. MUCH TALK MUCH WINE.)

Family Meeting On Liskeard Station

Suddenly we were all crying
You were dead -
No high-priest sang your requiem,
No huge sprays of flowers near your head -
Only us - your family alone
On a cold station
Waiting together for less than a second -
Before driving
All still crying
To the rest-house, where you
Were laid more silently
Than you had ever been.

Each one of us was quite separate -
Our thoughts betrayed our tears -
No great love for each other -
Only a kind of sympathy for
An aging widow'd mother
And a feeble tolerance of being
Brothers and sisters -
With a sorrow in our bowels -
A quiet anger for a family's mistakes
We could not spare too much pity -
But today was different -
You were dead now
Cold as white marble -
And you were our father
For better or worse -

Whatever stubborn curse follows us -
Directly flowing from your blood
Stream into our living circulation,
No black-devils could really
Out place that love for you
We all felt and shared and knew -
To be more than death's
Grinning sentiment -
More than 'blood's thicker than water' fable -
For we had shared your table
For a lifetime of quick laughter and bitter tears -
And your struggle with life -
Was maybe our salvation -
Now you are dead -
Your voice lingers on and on -

Down dozens of years -
Thro' deserted houses -
And in flashes from your grandson's tumbling words -

Suddenly
We'll cry forever -
Daddy cannot be re-discovered -

But somewhere – where
Time and place meet eternity -
That sweet man drinks strong tea
And plans, 'a comeback!'

Song Of The Red Sail

Sing me the tune of your eyes -
Sing me the hymn of your hands
Tell me in tumbling cries
Tell me I'll understand -

Pipe me along your walks -
Pipe me your soul's task -
Tell me in your talks
Tell me to drop the mask -

Strike up a song for Erato
Strike up a ditty for dreams -
Tuneful and loving it flows -
Tuneful and loving it seems -

A duet for an April breeze -
A duet about love and desire,
Sweet as the song from the trees -
Sweet as love's blue-fire -

Come waltz me along with your smile
Come waltz me over the sea -
For April is but a-while -
For love itself must flee -

So chant me the chirp of a bird -
So chant and whistle to me
For music is always heard -
For music sets lovers free -

Warble the songs of kings -
Warble the fables of old -
Together we'll laugh, we'll sing -
Together we'll not be cold -

So sing me the tune of your eyes -
Sing me the hymn of your hands -
Our love will always be wise
Our love will join sea to land -

Tell me in tumbling cries
Tell me I'll understand -
The sweet tune in your eyes -
The sweet dance of your hands -

Strum me a melody of wine -
Strum me a song of your hair -
Chant that today you are mine -
Chant that today we care -

A solo about sorrow -
A solo of parting and tears
No doubt you'll sing me tomorrow
No doubt you'll sing for years -

So pipe me along your heart -
So pipe me through your hair -
Sing me an apple-tree-tart -
Sing me a bright golden pear.

NECESSITAS
(FOR MY 57TH BIRTHDAY)

~~A terrible nothingness engulfs me~~
I am separated from all my hopes -
Aging, inhabits all my bones and bodily
I'm bound with scarlet pain, plaited like ropes -
Necessitas with her brazen hard nails
Decreed my fate and I am left captive -
Phantoms haunt my sleep and in my dreams wail,
United in their quest to hurt and jibe -
The wings of Liberty are beautiful
Her voice more lovely than music's echo -
She has the strength of a thousand great bulls -
All great rivers spring from Liberty's flow -

    From sorrow's aimless night, I will withdraw -
    As a thunderbolt of light strikes my door -

WINTER

Winter rain -
Thro' the mists
Again the phantoms come -
Hidden faces singing a melody
Of fading light,
A melancholy sun
Warms in small moments -

Splashes over glass -
Grey skies filled with winds -
Rain-wet trees shaking with
Their spirit strength -
Breaking leaves, fallen on damp grass,
Grieve at summer's passing -
And die at last -

Birds join the phantom's song
Knowing a year-long joy of flight
Now a bleak night of cold is theirs -
Storm will maul at feathers
Born of spring, ice will claim
A sacrifice of birds,
As heard only in echo
Of days gone, is their lovely song -

Earth with a jealous keeping -
Takes seed and root into herself -
Refusing all sign of precious fruit
Until, as it will always happen -
Spring seduced by hope, breaks
Open earth to flower and bee.

Man Is A Bundle Of Ash

Man is a bundle of ash
Tied in a kerchief of straw
Woven about him a sash
Taken from silk in the raw -

Man goes to war with the grin
Dies with a groan for a cause
Leaving behind such a din
From new and old-fashioned laws -

Man is a loose argument
Covered with simple truth
Nailed to a huge white tent
Housing a beautiful Ruth -

Man is dusty with sin
His world is a hat-full of lies
But somewhere between God and him
A Saint is born so wise -

And so it goes round in rhyme
A cycle of man's odd dreams
Where since the beginning of Time
Man comes apart at his seams -

Emily Brontë

On bleak Yorkshire nights -
As winter's air soured your broken chest -
Did you turn to your sisters and that brother
Who drunk and slightly mad - still make you smile -
Did you discover through them what it was like to love?

You were not touched by any man -
You were not passion-sucked or vain
With being loved - you were only ill and coughing -
When nights came with their mists and nightmares,
When hunters rode the moors and no lover's face
Invaded the room, where you spat blood -

But you loved more than anyone -
Who more than you knew of hands and fingers
Eyes and hair - who more than you could write
Lovers into pages taken from vales and hills
Of Yorkshire's wild winds and thick, black rain -

You more than your sisters understood
In so few years the heart's most secret beating -
Virgin and bothered with high fevers
You flowed always like some great river
Through the vales and mists of passion -
And by God you loved!

WHISPERS

Whispers my inner-self
To all I have become,
Where did you find the shelf
To hide from the one
Who you loved most?
Through ages of my heart's
Calling, calling to a ghost -
How weary, tired, cross love departs -
Leaving nothing, but a wrinkled brow -
Leaving nothing, but a falling tear -
Nobody ever tells me how
Or why true love must disappear -
   Yet I suppose there is a place
    Where my inner-self will find your face -

THE FADED LEAF

A faded leaf of friendship -
A changed ideal, a broken pattern -
A question being asked, an unbought birthday gift.
A dead child's memory filling the air -
A group of figures in silent prayer.

The gas fires in little houses
Deserted hearts beneath the pretty blouses
So this is youth grown stale -
Like a dog with worms behind its tail.

Onward, the cry is onward friends,
But, are you friends?
Is this the meaning of comradeship?
Stealing and lying,
Stride for stride,
Penny for penny -
Turn the playing-card over
Reach out for your grave!

Hark, it's Christmas again-
The blood near His name -
Like the holly-berry is bright-
The faded leaf falls like a broken kite.

Toys, we are all toys -
With broken pieces
Destruction of one friend or another -
The lover, the best pal, ones own brother -
Each made a perfect hole in the heart of a friend.
And in turn they were bitten and cried
Revenge - revenge - which brings us to
War.
The killing of surplus humanity, mingled
With a million friends, who died, because
They destroyed, then collapsed beneath
The burden of their sin.
War - friendship -
    There is but a subtle difference -

Change to a honey-bee
Live where flowers are prettily
Growing and dancing near the trees.
Let us all become honey-bees.

Away from this stench of superficial
~~Days and nights -~~
Months and years -
Parties and people
Race tracks and fools
Women - rags - and children's schools.
There is only a faint promise of
Faithfulness in a dead man and
Even his soul can betray you
Before his god.
Oh, Lord give us this day to find,
Not only bread, but
The evergreen leaf of eternity -
The gem more perfect than an
Emerald, on an ivory finger of a queen

>   Dancing to the moon's song -
>   Listening to the echo of a Chinese gong -
>   Footsteps and handshakes
>   The world of meretricious rapes -

Beckon you all to find a friend -
Have discourse and wine -
Intercourse and laughter
And the struggle, which inevitably
Follows after.
   And so be it -

A group of figures in silent prayer -
A dead child's memory filling the air -
An unbought birthday gift -
A question being asked -
A broken pattern, a changed ideal -
A faded leaf of friendship -

www.ingramcontent.com/pod-product-compliance
Lightning Source LLC
Chambersburg PA
CBHW051720040426
42446CB00008B/975